Richard Unglik's

SHERLOCK HOLMES
THE HOUND OF THE BASKERVILLES

A Playmobil interpretation
based on the story by
Sir Arthur Conan Doyle

Before we begin our story, allow us to introduce the main characters:

Metropolitan Police Service of London
SCOTLAND YARD
card-index number # 5847a14

CONFIDENTIAL

GENERAL INFORMATION

cattle shed on **Sherlock Holmes**

Name : HOLMES, Sherlock

Nationality : British
Born on :   1854
Residence :   221b Baker Street, London
Profession : Private detective

Size : average
Hair : brown
Eyes   brown

Distinguishing marks :

Usually wears a green deerstalker cap, a red
riding coat, and a gray cape.

SPECIFICS

- Is considered the best detective in London. Has
developed a method of investigation based on the
rigorous observation of people and facts, aided by
his rare powers of deduction and his encyclopedic
memory.
- Family situation: Single. Shares a flat with
Dr. James WATSON (File #3267b12), who acts as his
assistant. KEEP UNDER SURVEILLANCE.
-The medical practices of Dr. Watson have already
been seen as dangerous: using hallucinogens,
hypnosis, etc. KEEP UNDER SURVEILLANCE.
- They both have revolvers, a Colt 1836 each. KEEP
UNDER SURVEILLANCE.

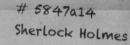

Private Detective
SHERLOCK HOLMES
221b Baker Street, London

5847a14
Sherlock Holmes

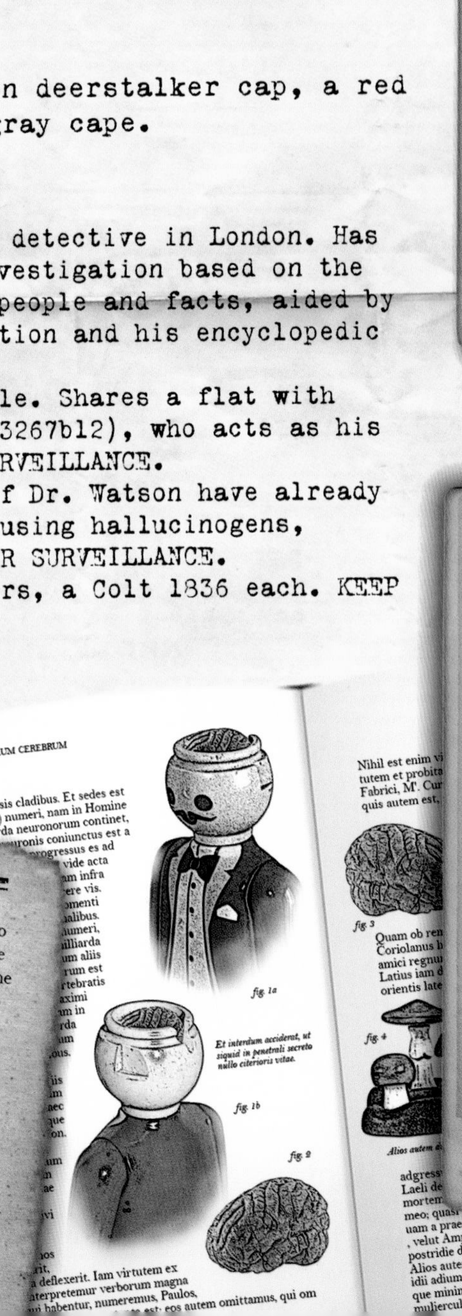

3267b12
Dr. Watson

PLAYMOBILUM CEREBRUM

ne haec sola pernicies orientem diversis cladibus. Et sedes est
rvalium (neuronorum) numeri, nam in Homine
100 milliarda neuronorum continet,
uronis coniunctus est a
ngressus es ad
vide acta
m infra
ere vis.
menti
alibus.
numeri,
milliarda
um aliis
rum est
rtebratis
aximi
am in
us.

fig 1a

Et interdum accidunt, ut
siquid in penetrali secreto
nullo citerioris vitae.

fig 1b

fig 2

Nihil est enim vi
tutem et probita
Fabrici, M. Cur
quis autem est,

fig 3

Quam ob rem
Coriolanus h
amici regnu
Latius iam d
orientis late

fig 4

Alios autem d

adgress
Laeli de
mortem
meo; quasi c
uam a praesentibus c
, velut Amphiarao re
postridie disceret im
Alios autem dicere a
que minimum firmitatis haberet minimumque
mulierculae magis amicitiarum praesidia quaerant quam viri et mop
beati

In 1836, Samuel Colt patented a revolver mechanism that led to
the widespread use of the revolver. According to Samuel Colt, he
came up with the idea for the revolver while at sea, inspired by the

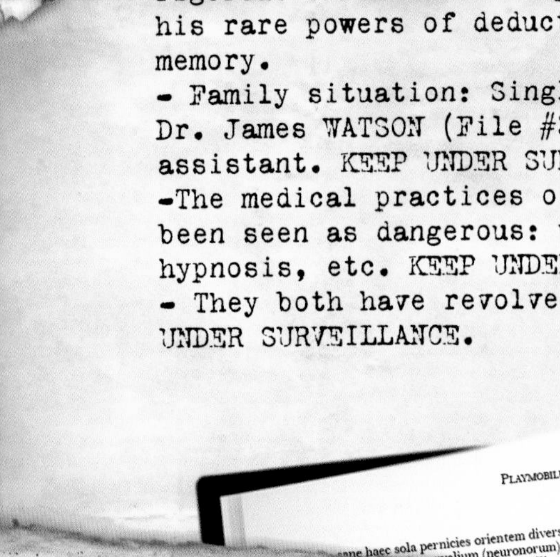

Revolver *Colt*, 1836

capstan winch, which had a ratchet and pawl mechanism on it, a
version of which was used in his

Death of Sir Charles Baskerville

The recent sudden death of Sir

speculation. More wise than those who go on until the wheel turns against them, he realized his gains

Sir Charles Baskerville

Sir Henry Baskerville

Huested · MANNSVILLE AND BELLEVILLE, N.Y.

Sir Charles Baskerville
A natural death or a curse on the family?

Hugo Baskerville, the wicked ancestor. Responsible for the terrible curse weighing on his family.

Sir Henry: Great-grandnephew of Sir Charles. The sole remaining heir of the Baskerville family.

Mr. & Mrs. Barrymore
Sir Charles's servants.
• Are they hiding something?
• Are they loyal servants or
   • scheming manipulators?

sir Hugo Baskerville

Sir Charles's doctor.
Dr. James MORTIMER

Sir Charles's physician thinks Sir Charles did not die of natural causes and asks Holmes to protect his heir.

Charing Cross Hospital, 1881

Quaerebatur hos...
POST OF...
Please Write Dist...

From: Dr. Mortimer, Grimpen, Devonshire

You have to attend to an important matter STOP

Our story begins one foggy evening as a thick
cloud falls upon the city.
At 221b Baker Street, Sherlock Holmes is in
his famous home.

SHERLOCK HOLMES AND THE HOUND OF THE BASKERVILLES

Chapter I
A VERY STRANGE AFFAIR

"Checkmate, my dear Watson," said Sherlock Holmes softly as he relit his pipe. Dr. Watson looked extremely surprised and, for a few seconds, his cup of tea hung in time and space. How could Sherlock Holmes be in such a position that he could beat him in five moves? Even after so many years of friendship, the immense brainpower of Sherlock Holmes was still a source of great wonder to Watson.

"And now, my dear friend," said Holmes, "would you be so kind as to tell me the time?"

"It's a quarter to six."

"Well, if the sender of the telegram I received a few days ago is punctual, we should be getting a visit soon."

Quaerebatur hos

POST

From: Dr. Mortimer, Gri
Devonshire

You must attend

Arrive late afte

Dr. James MORTIMER

Member of the Royal College of Surgeons
Former Intern of the Charing Cross Hospital

Medical Officer of Grimpen, Dartmoor

He lived a healthy and active life, with regular trips to the countryside.

rmorum manus industria nec e aliquotiens ostendens ab.

ICE TELEGRAPHS

No. of message

ite Distinctly

To: Sherlock Holmes,
221b Baker Street, London

ortant case STOP

November 4th STOP

And, as if replying to the detective's words, the doorbell rang.

"Do come in!"

The man crossed the doorway, bowed politely, and introduced himself.

"Doctor Mortimer, James Mortimer."
"I am delighted to make the acquaintance of the most famous detective and his inseparable assistant, the equally famous Dr. Watson."

"The pleasure is all ours," replied Sherlock Holmes, who was used to this kind of praise.

"And now, my dear sir, would you be so kind as to tell us the purpose of your visit?"

"I've come all the way from Devon," began Dr. Mortimer, "to tell you about the death of Sir Charles Baskerville, which you might have heard something about."

"Indeed, I remember reading about it in the papers," replied Sherlock Holmes.

Upon this remark, Dr. Mortimer pulled out a copy of the *Daily Mail* dated October 17th. He unfolded it with care, turned a few pages, and after clearing his throat, began reading the article about the death of Sir Charles Baskerville.

THE DAILY MAIL

JEAN MICHEL COBLENCE
FOUNDER

FOR KING AND EMPIRE WITH PLAYMOBIL

MCXXIXVIII
OCTOBER 17TH 1888

JACK THE RIPPER STRIKES AGAIN!

The body of a woman named Mary Ann Nichols was discovered two nights ago on a street in Whitechapel, one of London's poorest areas. The middle-aged woman was found with her throat cut. This murder, attributed to Jack the Ripper, will increase the terror on the streets of London. An

Mary Anne Nichols
Nickname: "Polly"

Annie Chapman
Nickname: "Dark Annie"

Elizabeth Stride
Nickname: "Long Liz"

Catherine Eddowes
Nickname: "Kate Conway"

inquiry was opened by coroner Wynne Baxter, a civil servant. This savage murder is causing much fear among the population, as there is no witness, no weapon, and no evidence. In short, there are no leads at all to begin solving this mystery. It is no surprise that the inhabitants of Whitechapel are noting similarities between this event and the other recent gruesome murders, and panic is starting to grip the general public.

Rumor has it that a man nicknamed "Leather Apron" has been attacking women in order to steal their money. Our fellow newspaper, *The Times of London*, thinks they have identified an unknown man, relatively large, with a moustache, and wearing a hat and large boots.

The police have made the link to another case, as a woman's body was discovered the same night in a small backyard close to Spitalfields Market. The unfortunate woman, who was named Annie Chapman, had been stabbed. Despite the presence of a number of vendors in the market, nobody heard or saw anything. Mrs. Chapman was a homeless woman, aged 47. A widow, she had two children and no money, and had fallen on hard times. When the doctor arrived, he discovered a grisly scene. The

victim was almost beheaded and sliced open. The cuts were extremely precise, indicating that the perpetrator had a good knowledge of anatomy. Once more, the inquiry is at a dead end. Without wanting to scare the reader, we remind you that two other women, Elizabeth Stride and Catherine Eddowes, were also viciously murdered and mutilated in a similar fashion.

Across the whole of London, rumors are spreading, along with anger against the police. People are now avoiding the borough of Whitechapel at night. Accusations are flying and fear is rampant in the East End. While most inhabitants are shocked, as is always the case with such incidents, others are writing to the police claiming to be the killer. Two letters have caught the attention of the police, both written by the same person and signed "Jack the Ripper." They give troubling details about the last two murders and refer to an older case, the murder of Mary Jane Kelly, nicknamed "Ginger," a tavern girl found dead on the banks of the Thames. The policemen are now tangled in their own investigations. They are currently interviewing witnesses and are trying to sort their statements. Some are very precise, while others are clearly made up. A high-ranking officer, Sir Charles Warren, the Chief Inspector at Scotland Yard, is convinced that the use of sniffer dogs could help the police find leads to the sinister murderer. It is said that such training for the dogs is already underway and that bloodhounds are discreetly being brought to Whitechapel.

(Continued on page 2)

ANGER AT BUCKINGHAM PALACE

There are reports that even Queen Victoria herself is very upset by this series of crimes and has ordered that each and every street in London be equipped with public lighting. Ironically, the case of Jack the Ripper is bringing light to this rundown borough in our

capital city, considered the most beautiful in the world. Can we hope that, one day, the slums will be demolished, the streets lit, and the orphans taken care of? Will the East End one day be completely transformed? One remembers the emotional depictions of poverty by the famous writer Charles Dickens in his novel *Oliver Twist*. That book was published 50 years ago! Has the situation improved? The truth, unfortunately, is that it has not!

Summoned to the palace by our gracious queen, the prime minister went home after an hour-long meeting. No comment has been made about the discussions taking place at the highest level of the kingdom, though Parliament opposed a plan to interrogate the government about their responsibilities during the next session in the House of Commons.

THE DEATH OF SIR CHARLES BASKERVILLE

The recent passing of Sir Charles Baskerville saddened the entire town of Grimpen in Devon.

His kindness and generosity had won him the respect and affection of all who knew him. A widower without a direct heir, Sir Charles made sure the farms and villages nearby benefited from his great fortune, and many charities have reason to mourn him.

We must mention the troubled circumstances of Sir Charles's death. According to the superstition of local people, Sir Charles is the latest victim in a family tragedy known in the area as the curse of the Hound of the Baskervilles.

Despite this rumor, nothing indicates any other conclusion than that he died of natural causes. Sir Charles's body showed no sign of violence or any wounds.

Sir Charles Baskerville

Several trustworthy witnesses, including the deceased's own physician, Dr. Mortimer, and his servants, Mr. and Mrs. Barrymore, stated that Sir Charles suffered from cardiac problems. This was confirmed by the autopsy, which revealed a severe cardiovascular condition. According to the coroner, this is the likely cause of death.

The county police agree with this explanation and are ignoring the villagers' highly superstitious accounts of the appearance of a monstrous, ghostly dog.

According to our local correspondent, who sought to interview them, neither the eminent doctor nor Major Harrison,

The ruins of the Abbey of Grimpen, where the body of Sir Charles was found.

the local chief of police, have made any public statement or given any comment, due to the ongoing investigation and the social status of the deceased. There is a widespread hope that the investigation won't go any further, as it is of the utmost importance that an heir settles quickly in Baskerville in order to resume Sir Charles's charity work.

The closest family member to the victim is reported to be a distant nephew named Henry Baskerville.

He currently lives in America, and a search was launched to inform him of his new fortune.

(Continued on page 6)

THE GREAT RISE OF THE DEPARTMENT STORE

Already well known to our city readers, department stores are multiplying, in London of course, but also in Leeds, Manchester, Birmingham, Liverpool, Glasgow, and Edinburgh. The small, medieval shops in dark alleys are slowly being replaced by major retailers offering multiple locations, with a better supply and restocking of their products. These new stores allow one to shop peacefully, safe from the rain and chaotic traffic. Going hand-in-hand with the emergence of the middle class and its spending power, these stores label their products with fixed prices, which puts an end to haggling. Their lower margins are balanced by a high volume of business, which ensures good prices. All this allows them to broadcast their many offers and sales, which change regularly and are promoted by advertisements, sale periods, home deliveries, mail orders, and returns. A symbol of this new business structure, the huge Harrods store on Brompton Road in the borough of Knightsbridge was recently refurbished in its entirety. Five years ago, on December 6th, 1883, a terrible fire burned the shop, created by Charles Digby Harrod, to ashes. Despite this disaster, the storeowner still managed to honor all the orders for that year and the next year, after settling the business in a temporary building. After many years of work, the new Harrods has now arrived! Even bigger and more beautiful than the last one, and entirely lit by electricity, it will excite even the most demanding customers. All the latest fashions from Paris can be found there, as well as all the hats, bonnets, and accessories one needs to be admired in good society.

Dr. Mortimer was about to continue reading the *Daily Mail* when Sherlock Holmes interrupted him.

"Pardon me, doctor, but I assume you didn't come all the way from Devonshire to read us an article that, whilst I'm sure would fascinate a local of Grimpen, contains nothing that could justify the attention of a criminologist like me. In order to better understand, could you please tell us in your own words the reason for your visit?"

"Quite so," conceded Mortimer, while folding the paper. "I was Sir Charles's friend as much as his doctor, which is why the topic upsets me. Sir Charles was a gentleman in every sense of the word. The only passion I ever knew him to have was for flowers. He took great care of them in the winter garden he built in one of the only sunny spots in Baskerville Hall. It is, I must say, the only part of the manor that doesn't feel like a haunted castle!

"Sir Charles spent all his evenings in the winter garden. At 10 o'clock sharp his maid, Mrs. Barrymore, would serve him a cup of tea and the medication I prescribed him for his very fragile heart. He usually went to his room immediately afterward.

"On the night of October 14th, the maid arrived at 10 o'clock as usual, but was surprised when she didn't find him there. She became more concerned when she noticed that the small doorway to the manor was opened."

"Why was she so worried? Did it not occur to her that Sir Charles might go and have a stroll on the moor?"

"During the day, certainly!" replied Mortimer. Then, lowering his voice as if he was telling a secret:

"... but Sir Charles would never have gone to the moor on his own at night."

"What makes you so certain?"

"The moor terrified him."

As Sherlock Holmes and Dr. Watson were watching him, perplexed, Dr. Mortimer withdrew a document from his case.

"Here is a manuscript that Sir Charles entrusted to me personally. It is the story of the legend that has been told for generations in the Baskerville family."

"Is it the same as the legend mentioned in the papers?"

"The very same. It is the story of the evil ancestor, Sir Hugo Baskerville, who died on the moor as he chased an innocent young woman. The legend explains that Sir Hugo and the young woman were attacked in the middle of the night by a monstrous dog that came straight from the mouth of hell. The story implores the descendants of Sir Hugo to never, ever go out on the moor at night again."

While Sherlock Holmes and Dr. Watson examined the curious document, Mortimer continued.

"Over the past few months, I had noticed that Sir Charles's nerves were greatly affected. He seemed extremely anxious and sometimes on the verge of collapse. This legend so terrified him that, despite the pleasure he took in strolling on his land, nothing would ever have persuaded him to go out at night on the moor! He was convinced that there was a terrible curse on his family. The idea of a ghostly presence haunted him. More than once, he asked me whether in the course of my visits or as I was leaving Baskerville, I had heard groans or howls on the moor."

"A difficult admission for a man of science like you, I should imagine," said Sherlock Holmes. "But let me finish reading this strange manuscript."

The Legend of the Curse of the Baskervilles

Hear the tale of the curse of the Hound of the Baskervilles.
In the dark year of 1642, Sir Hugo Baskerville was living in his manor. He was a wild character, vicious, harmful, and according to some, like the devil himself!

Such was his cruelty that the mere mention of his name filled the country with dread.

Sir Hugo Baskerville !

Now, as it happened, Sir Hugo fell in love with a young woman from the village.

The young woman took great pains to avoid him, as she was afraid of his horrible reputation. One winter evening, Sir Hugo, along with some partners in crime, kidnapped the young woman and locked her in the castle attic.

The poor young woman was terrified by the singing and swearing that came from the main hall where the men were having a good time. Though she was frightened, she opened the window, escaped from the castle, and raced across the moor in the middle of the night.

Sir Hugo flew into a rage when he realized his prisoner was gone. His eyes turned black with anger and, as if possessed by a demon, he swore to his friends that before dawn he would find the young woman.

He mounted his horse and rushed out into the mist that covered the moor. What happened next, no living soul would ever know.

Hugo never returned to the castle. Two bodies were found the next day beside the ruins of the old abbey: first, the young woman, frightened to death; the other, Sir Hugo, torn to shreds by the claws and teeth of a monstrous dog.

Never venture alone to the moor at night, when the demons run wild! Beware!

You could meet the creature from hell:
the Hound of the Baskervilles!

"It's certainly a strange tale," said Sherlock Holmes. "But, Dr. Mortimer, what makes you think that Sir Charles's death could have anything to do with these tales from the dim and distant past?"

"I'm coming to that, Mr. Holmes. When his wife told him about the disappearance of his master, Barrymore left the manor and went looking for him. It had rained that day, and Sir Charles had left clear footprints behind him. They led straight to the ruins of the old Abbey of Grimpen, to the exact spot where, according to the legend, Hugo the Wicked had been torn to pieces by the hell-hound. And it is precisely there that Barrymore found the lifeless body of Sir Charles!

"Alerted by Mrs. Barrymore, I quickly arrived at the scene of the tragedy. Unfortunately, there was nothing I could do for poor Sir Charles but declare him dead. I saw no signs of violence on his body... But his face, good lord, his face!

"Never had I seen such deformation. It was obviously the most acute case of dyspnea I had seen in my entire career."

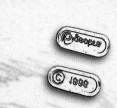

"Dyspnea?" Holmes interrupted him.

"It is a respiratory obstruction caused by a sudden acceleration of the heartbeat," explained Dr. Watson. "It is a common risk for people suffering from heart disease."

"Of course, that was to be expected," Dr. Mortimer went on. "But something caught my attention: the footsteps appeared different, as if Sir Charles had suddenly been walking on his toes, as if he was sneaking up on something or someone."

Dr. Mortimer sighed deeply before continuing. It was clear he was reluctant to say certain words.

"Not only that, there were other footprints beside those of Sir Charles..."

"Of a man or woman?" asked Holmes.

Dr. Mortimer came closer to the detective, closed his eyes, and said in a muffled voice:

"Those footsteps belonged to a hound, Mr. Holmes. A MONSTROUS HOUND! A GIGANTIC HOUND!"

Seeing how distressed Dr. Mortimer had become, Watson could not suppress a shiver of anguish. Holmes had more self-control, though he was certainly intrigued by this new development.

"Did you see these footprints with your own eyes?"

"As clearly as I see you now."

"Could you have mistaken them for the footsteps of a sheepdog or a stray?" suggested Dr. Watson.

"The size of these footprints suggest the hound was as big as an exotic beast," replied Mortimer. "I assure you, gentlemen, they did not match any animal normally found in our country."

"Why isn't this mentioned in the newspaper article?" asked Holmes.

"I am the only one who saw those prints, Mr. Holmes. They were about 30 feet from the body. When the police arrived the next morning, they had been washed away by the rain and could no longer be seen. I must confess that if I hadn't been aware of the legend, I might have ignored them myself."

"Well then, why not mention them to the police?"

Dr. Mortimer paused briefly before replying.

"Well, I didn't want Baskerville Hall to be tarnished by the rumors of a curse or by superstitions. You need to understand, dear sirs, that the heir to Baskerville lives in peace in America where he enjoys his fortune. I wouldn't want the rumors to scare him off so badly that he doesn't come back to live in the castle of his ancestors..."

"I understand," replied Holmes. "Please remind me of his name."

"Henry, Sir Henry Baskerville. He arrived in London yesterday, and we have an appointment tomorrow at his hotel. I must confess that I am a little apprehensive of the meeting. If this case is of any interest to you, would you mind accompanying me?"

"I don't have much spare time, but I must admit that my curiosity is piqued," replied Sherlock Holmes. "Dr. Watson and I will be there."

Sir Henry Baskerville

The next day, toward the end of the morning, Holmes and Watson hailed a carriage and quietly settled in to enjoy the journey to the Saint James Hotel.

The streets of the capital were jam-packed, and the traffic made it difficult to move. The wheelbarrows, wagons, and horse-drawn carriages of the middle class, the carriages of the upper class, the postal trunks, the buses and firefighter carriages... Everybody was rushing around on the cobblestone streets.

Chapter II
SIR HENRY BASKERVILLE

When Sherlock Holmes and Watson arrived at Sir Henry's suite at the Saint James Hotel, Dr. Mortimer was already there. He made the introductions.

"Well, gentlemen, if it is as Dr. Mortimer claims, and I am in the presence of the finest detective in London, I'm sure you'll take no time at all to explain what seems to me to be a practical joke."

His sarcastic tone betrayed a barely contained anger, of which Sherlock Holmes couldn't understand the source.

"Which practical joke are you talking about?" asked Holmes.

"The theft of my hat! I just bought it at Harrods. You'll understand that my American wardrobe is not suitable for an English gentleman. Anyway, while I was at the reception desk sending a telegram, someone came in here and took my hat!"

"Is it not the gray hat laying on the pedestal table?" asked Holmes. "It looks like it's brand new and appears to be from Harrods."

"Exactly!" replied Sir Henry.

"So it wasn't stolen!"

"As I came downstairs to complain about the theft, the practical joker came back into my room and laid the hat down on this pedestal table."

"So, everything is fine then!" exclaimed Mortimer, relieved at this outcome. "The thief must have had a sudden pang of remorse. Or else the hat did not fit his head."

"Well, no," replied Sir Henry. "Following the removal of the hat, a slipper was also stolen from me. I might have understood if they'd taken a pair, but just one slipper... You'll forgive me, dear sirs, but the customs in this country seem very strange to me!"

He then turned to Mortimer:

"You had the kindness, dear doctor, to warn me of some mysterious dangers troubling my family."

"I am aware, of course, of the ghastly story of my ancestor Hugo; it was told to me on more than one occasion as a child. But am I to believe that this terrible Hound of the Baskervilles is, in fact, a beastly slipper thief?"

As they were talking, a huge spider discreetly crawled out of the hat. Having scuttled across the pedestal table, it was now climbing up Sir Henry's back.

"For the love of god, Sir Henry, don't move! Your life is in danger!" warned Sherlock Holmes.

The creeping spider had now reached the shoulders of the Baskerville heir. Its hairy legs were almost stroking his neck... Sweat was beading on Sir Henry's temples. His heart was beating very fast.

Holmes grabbed Dr. Mortimer's cane and, in a single precise movement, swiped the spider onto the floor and crushed it under his foot.

Calmly, Dr. Watson leaned over what remained of the spider.

"African tarantula. Its venom isn't deadly."

"It is nonetheless alarming enough to startle the most courageous of men," added Holmes for the benefit of Sir Henry. "Especially for a man with heart problems such as yourself."

Sir Henry was close to fainting. He dropped onto the bed and Dr. Mortimer served him a glass of brandy to calm his nerves.

Upon more closely examining the hat from which the spider had emerged, Holmes discovered a small piece of paper that he unfolded carefully.

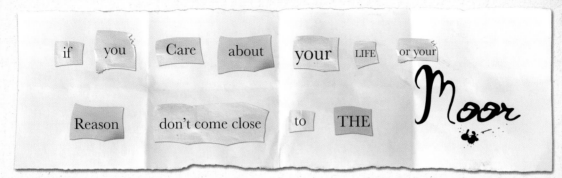

"Somebody is very keen to see that you don't visit the moor, Sir Henry."
Then, turning to Mortimer:
"Who knew the date of Sir Henry's arrival at the Saint James Hotel?"
"No one, aside from Sir Henry and myself. I only mentioned this hotel once to Sir Henry in a letter as I was preparing for his arrival in London."
"I never mentioned this hotel to anyone," the shocked nobleman agreed.
"Then someone followed you here," concluded Sherlock Holmes.
After thinking for a few seconds, he added:
"Luckily, this message gives us plenty of information about the perpetrator. Clearly, he does not want to harm you; but the presence of a spider with the message leads me to think that this is more of a threat than a friendly warning.

"I would add that it is someone you know or that you will meet soon. He is educated, determined... and visibly in a hurry. He doesn't appear to live in London.
"I can also say that he is left-handed."
"You can deduce all this from a simple anonymous message?" asked Sir Henry, plainly incredulous.
"It is my job, sir. It is how one must apply scientific imagination: always have a material basis for one's speculations."

"Now, examine this message carefully," continued Holmes. "You will admit that a man whose handwriting was unknown to Sir Henry would hardly take the precaution of writing his message with newspaper clippings. I said he was an educated person. Why? Because these clippings were cut out of *The Times*—the fonts are easily recognizable—and not from one of those popular newspapers.

"Last, but not least, I said that the author of this mysterious threat was determined and in a hurry. How could it be otherwise, since you have been in London for less than a day?

"Now, look carefully: the words are not aligned with precision. Negligence? Haste or irritation? I would definitely say the former. Indeed, I can assert that the message was crafted this very day, from a fascinating article I read in *The Times* this morning."

Before his incredulous audience, Sherlock Holmes asked Watson to read aloud the article in question.

Holding the newspaper, Watson did as instructed, pausing with admiration at the relevant words: "If"... "Care"... "Your life"..."Don't come close"...

Care

If   out   your   LIFE   or your

don't come close   to   THE   *Moor*

"Mr. Holmes, this goes beyond everything I had imagined!" exclaimed Mortimer. "That you are able to recall the precise words from an article you read this morning in the papers, it is remarkable! What an incredible memory!"

"Once again, my dear doctor, these are the core principles of my specialty. Now, let us examine the word 'Moor.' It is handwritten because, as you will agree, it is not an easy word to find in a newspaper. This is a stroke of fortune, as the handwritten word teaches us two things: first, it is the handwriting of a man; and second, that the man is likely not from London, as it was written in a hotel room."

"Good Heavens, Mr. Holmes, I cannot wait to hear how you have arrived at this conclusion!" exclaimed Sir Henry.

"Please have a close look at the word 'Moor.' The quill dried twice in the space of this short word. So the quill was secondhand and the inkwell almost empty...a recurrent problem for inkwells found in hotels.

"Now, take another look at the other groups of words, bearing my hypothesis in mind. Look at the curve of the cut: they were cut with nail scissors, the sort that you would find in a hotel room. And the curve of the clippings show, without the shadow of a doubt, that we are dealing with a left-handed man."

"Extraordinary!" exclaimed Mortimer. To show that he too could contribute to the inquiry, the doctor added:
     "We also know that our man specialized in exotic spiders."
     "Not necessarily," Holmes interrupted. "There are a number of shops in London, accessible to anyone, that specialize in the trade of potentially dangerous animals."

     He turned to Watson:
     "My dear friend, could you find the time, between two games of bridge, to go and question the shop owners of Bloomsbury Street on this particular matter?"
"But of course. I shall go tomorrow."

Sherlock Holmes moved closer to the Baskerville heir.
     "Now, Sir Henry, I'd like to know your intentions."
     "What do you mean?"
     "Do you think it is a good idea to go to Baskerville Hall?"
     "Why not?"
     "Because real dangers could await you there."
     "Do you mean danger from a hell-hound or from other human beings?"
     "That's precisely what we need to discover."
     "It doesn't matter. My answer will be the same. There is no infernal creature, let alone a mere human being, that can prevent me from returning to my ancestral home. I depart in three days for Devon."
     "Sir Henry, you are as brave a man as I could hope to meet! Some important matters will detain me in London for the coming weeks, but Dr. Watson will travel with you and keep me informed. For the time being, gentlemen, I must say goodbye and return to my office."

Chapter III
SHERLOCK HOLMES'S THOUGHTS

Back on Baker Street, Sherlock Holmes retreated into silence, much as Dr. Watson had expected. He knew that silence and solitude were indispensable to his friend during these hours of intense focus. Holmes was weighing every fact, every clue, every witness statement. He evaluated them and separated the essential details from the trivial facts.

Dr. Watson settled into an armchair with a glass of brandy and immersed himself in a book about the capacity of the human brain that had been fascinating him the past couple of days.

The day passed in this manner, studiously, quietly. When the clock struck at tea time, Holmes hadn't said a word.
The sound of his voice made Watson jump.

"There are two questions that need to be answered. First, did Sir Charles die a natural death, or was he the victim of a crime?
"Second, if a crime was committed, how was it committed, and who committed it?
"I set aside the third hypothesis, made by Dr. Mortimer, which accepts the intervention of a supernatural being, as this would render our inquiry redundant.
"That being said, some of the details are certainly strange. The footprints that changed shape on the ground, for instance. Your opinion, Watson?"

"Dr. Mortimer said that Sir Charles walked down the stairs on his toes."
"Indeed! But why would a man go down the stairs in such a fashion?"

Watson remained silent as Sherlock Holmes went on:

"He was running, Watson! He was running desperately; he was running to save his life, until his fragile heart exploded and he dropped dead!"

"Indeed! But why would a man run down the stairs?"

"What was he running from? It can't be a dog. Even a large one couldn't provoke such panic. Next," Holmes went on, "why was Sir Charles alone on the moor in the dead of night when, according to Mortimer, he was both aware of and frightened by the old horrors surrounding the legend of the Baskervilles? He must have been coaxed there by someone or something."

Holmes lit a pipe and moved his armchair closer to Watson's.

"We won't learn a thing more by remaining here in London, my dear Watson. You must go with Sir Henry and Dr. Mortimer and try to unknot the threads of this mystery. Be very careful, my dear friend, it is a most dangerous affair; the more I think about it, the less I like it.

"As I said, I am tied up in London with some clients, but I would like to receive regular updates from Devon. And I will be glad to see you back soon, safe and sound, on Baker Street."

Wednesday, November 6ᵗʰ, 1888

A pleasant journey to Devon, in spite of the gloomy weather. Train to Southampton where we embark on the Lily-Jane. Peaceful sea.

I take the opportunity to learn more about my traveling companion.

Sir Henry is a surprising character, active and determined. He also loves being a social figure and certainly appreciates the company of women.

During our journey, one young lady in particular caught his attention; a Miss Pinson, a pretty French lady who has come to England to perfect her command of our language.

They didn't leave each other's side for the whole crossing!

As we did not fancy ourselves as chaperones, Dr. Mortimer and I admired the wondrous mechanism of the steamboat — one of our century's great inventions!

Devonshire

Grimpen

Baskerville Hall

Moor of Dartmoor

Plymouth

Thursday, November 7ᵗʰ

Arrived in Plymouth in the middle of the afternoon. A carriage driven by a man named Perkins was waiting to drive us to Baskerville Hall.

After Sir Henry said his farewells to Miss Pinson, the three men climbed into Perkins's carriage. After an hour, Dr. Mortimer stopped the car at the crossing of a road and asked that he be left there. He explained he had a patient to attend to and that he would lose time by going all the way to Baskerville Hall.

"Dr. Mortimer, I advise you against crossing the moor at this hour," said Perkins.
"And I advise you to wait until someone asks you to speak, Perkins!" Mortimer retorted.

Sir Henry intervened, "What do you mean, Perkins? Is our friend in danger?"
"A dangerous criminal called Selden escaped from the county prison the day before yesterday. Everything leads us to believe that he is hiding somewhere on the moor."

"Come now, do not worry. I know these moors like the back of my hand, and I am capable of defending myself..."
And with these words, Dr. Mortimer set out on the path to Grimpen as the carriage continued on its way to Baskerville Hall.

Chapter IV
ARRIVAL AT BASKERVILLE HALL

On a moonless night in a swirling fog the travelers finally reached the gates of Baskerville Hall. A gloomy person would have compared the arrival to a funeral procession arriving at an isolated countryside cemetery.

The new owner of the estate cast gloomy glances at the scene, looking for a reason to be cheerful, some detail to be excited about. Though he was a strong-minded man, he couldn't help but shiver at the sight of his ancestors' manor as it rose out of the mist like a ghost ship.

"It doesn't surprise me that my dear uncle was prone to such dark thoughts! This is enough to disturb even the most fearless soul. Give me three months and I'll arrange a row of street lights!"

The manor appeared deserted.
 "Is there nobody to welcome us?" muttered Sir Henry.
Despite his usual calmness, Dr. Watson shared his host's anxiety.
And his worries intensified as he spotted a silhouette watching them from an attic window.

Barely had Perkins stopped the carriage in front of the manor, when the heavy oak door creaked open. A pale man appeared, a torch in his hand. It was Barrymore, the butler.

"Welcome to Baskerville Hall, sirs."
Then, turning to Sir Henry:
"Welcome home, sir."

As Sir Henry and Dr. Watson stepped down from the carriage, Perkins carried their luggage to the door. Then, without waiting for thanks or a tip, he said his goodbyes, cracked his whip, and left the premises.

Barrymore invited Sir Henry and Dr. Watson to come inside and warm up.
"Dinner will be served as soon as sir wishes. Meanwhile, allow me to take you to your rooms. There you will find your luggage and some hot water." Then he added, as if answering the question Sir Henry had been about to ask:
"My wife sends her apologies. She is not feeling well but will come downstairs and welcome you shortly."

Dinner was served a short while later in the castle's great hall. Mrs. Barrymore took the opportunity to come and greet the new master. Her welcoming words, however, were as brief as they were cold. After serving a thick soup and some potatoes, she disappeared as quickly as she had entered.

Barrymore stepped in:

"I beg you, sir, to forgive my wife. We were both very fond of Sir Charles, and his passing has upset us greatly. Living in this house is now a great burden, and I'm afraid we'll never feel comfortable being here."

"Am I to understand that you wish to retire from my service?"

"My wife and I will be happy to serve you until you've found new staff. Once you have done so, we'll leave and set up a small business in a shop."

"You are, of course, free to make your own decisions. But I know that your family has been in the service of mine for generations. I should be sorry to begin my time in Baskerville by cutting loose an old family bond."

The butler could not hide his sorrow. Making hasty excuses, he vanished toward the kitchen, leaving the two guests sitting beneath the silent gaze of all the ancestors of Baskerville.

"My word, this place does not make the heart sing," said Sir Henry to break the silence.

"Indeed. Though, this is exactly as I imagined it," replied Watson. "Isn't it just the perfect vision of an old haunted house overrun by ghostly ancestors? I'll probably get used to it. But it certainly isn't any wonder that my uncle became so... jumpy, living on his own in such a place."

They exchanged a few more words and then, dinner being finished, both headed back to their rooms, hoping the night air would blow away the sinister atmosphere.

Their first night at Baskerville did not bring the rest they were hoping for. Dr. Watson, in particular, struggled to fall asleep. He tossed and turned in his bed as if he were expecting something to happen. The manor was engulfed by silence. But suddenly, in the deepest dark of the night, Watson heard the unmistakable noise of a woman shrieking and sobbing.

Watson sat up in bed and listened carefully. The barely stifled wails came without a doubt from a woman troubled by something terrible and violent and rose to an almost uncontrollable panic.

Why was Mrs. Barrymore—for who else could it be—in a state of such distress?

Watson rose from his bed and lit the gas lamp. As he paced up and down his room, through the window he spotted a light flickering out on the moor near the ruins of the old abbey.

What was going on? Was someone out there in the middle of the night?

Before long the crying stopped, the light on the moor vanished, and the manor was silent again. Eventually, even Dr. Watson managed to fall asleep...

In the silence of Baskerville Hall, Watson's sleep was disturbed by a succession of

STRANGE DREAMS...

BILL THE BUTCHER

The Good Cake

Apothecary

Watson had made up his mind to walk all the way to the village of Grimpen. Before starting his inquiry, and because he was starving, he stopped at the The Good Cake bakery to sample the blueberry muffins. Someone had recommended the place to him and, as a man who loved good food, he was not disappointed.

The
Good Cake

Tea and Pastry

Founded in 1882

The Good Cake

The following morning, the doctor met Sir Henry for breakfast.
He had also heard noises during the night, but dismissed them as a bad dream and
fell asleep again quite easily. He questioned Barrymore on the matter.

The butler seemed a little uncomfortable at the question and claimed he had not
heard or seen anything out of the ordinary. After breakfast, as Sir Henry set out on
a tour of his property, Watson unpacked
his Remington typewriter to compose his
first report to Sherlock Holmes.

Name: SELDEN, Robert   D.R. # 999047

Age: 26 (when rec'd)

DOB: 01

County:

Age at

Weight:

Native

My dear Holmes,

Let me report on my first impressions of Baskerville.
First, as if the moors didn't offer danger enough, we hear that Selden, the Notting
Hill murderer, escaped only a few days ago and is probably hiding out there. You
will find details on this in the newspaper article attached.

Our arrival in Baskerville
Hall itself was not pleasant;
in fact, far from it. To tell
the truth, I have the distinct
impression we are not welcome
here.
Extremely reluctant to
accompany us to the manor,
Dr. Mortimer left us along the
way before our arrival and
only Mr. and Mrs. Barrymore
were in attendance to welcome
Sir Henry and me.
A decidedly strange couple!
Polite and courteous,
certainly, but almost as pale, muted,
and sinister as the rest of our surroundings. Mr. Barrymore has already
explained that the death of Sir Charles has affected them so much that they can
no longer imagine continuing their service to the Baskerville family.

That said, they have offered to stay for as long as it takes Sir Henry to find
suitable replacements.
After that, they plan to open a shop in town with the savings that Sir Charles
left them in his will.
No specific incidents occurred at dinner, and then everybody retired to bed.
As you know, I am prone to insomnia, and despite my exhaustion, I was still wide
awake at 3 o'clock in the morning, when I clearly heard someone sobbing. Two things
are certain:

1) It was a woman crying.
2) The crying came from within the manor.

I, therefore, presume that it must have been Mrs. Barrymore.

This morning, after breakfast, I asked Barrymore whether his wife had been feeling
unwell and if she had cried during the night. He assured me that she had not.
But as I walked back toward the living room, I crossed paths with Mrs. Barrymore
in the corridor. Her eyes were red and swollen. In my opinion, there is no doubt that
this woman had been crying.

Why would Barrymore lie to me?

What is he trying to hide? I know how much, my dear Holmes, you are suspicious of hasty reasoning, and how much you avoid jumping to conclusions. Through you, I have learned to examine each and every fact of a case and base my reasoning on clearly established truths only. And yet, if we are to conclude that Sir Charles's death was not natural, but criminal, I cannot hide from you how heavily my suspicions would fall upon on this man!

I will add that, in pursuit of further knowledge, I have tried discreetly to search the manor. But it is impossible! Most of the doors are locked, and for those that are open, I can't come close without Barrymore or his wife suddenly appearing from who-knows-where and asking me what I am looking for or whether they can be of any assistance…

This taste for concealment is not to my liking at all.

In order to escape this oppressive atmosphere, I have made another decision: I will walk immediately to the village of Grimpen. I shall post this report I addressed to you and shall investigate the knowledge of the shop owners and local inhabitants. I wish to hear their thoughts on the old lord of the manner, his servants, and of course, their view of the mysterious legend of the Hound of the Baskervilles. I will also try to unearth more about Selden, the escaped fugitive, as the possibility of his presence in the area is unsettling.

I intend to keep you informed as often as I can. Until then, kindest regards from Devon, a place that still holds many secrets from me!

Your devoted servant,
Watson

Drawings based on descriptions by John Cook.

fig b

fig c

us industria nec e aliquotiens ostendens ab.

TELEGRAPHS   No. of message

tly

To: DR. WATSON

ISTANCE
MOOR ALONE STOP

them in flight in low-light situati...

fig b

...done to dispose of those rumours to which local superstition has given rise.

There is no reason whatever to suspect foul play, or to imagine that death could...

The witness statement of John Cook, traveling book merchant.

A regular traveler along the roads of Devon. He claims that one night he saw an animal that, as he assured me, was not a wolf but a "glowing beast."

Post-man

Grimpen, 1888

Mary Aliscott, nicknamed "Old Mary."

Apothecary
Bakery
Butcher
Main Street
Little river
Jeweler
dr Mortimer
wood
to ...erville Hall
to the moor

Grimpen, November 10th, 1888.

I decided first to go to the post office to send my report to Sherlock Holmes. The old devil had already sent me a surprise: a telegram stating that in no case was I to let Sir Henry venture alone onto the moor...

I then continued my tour of the peaceful streets of this little Devonshire town and talked to the shop owners as I went by. The butcher didn't tell me much. Knowing that Selden, the escaped convict, was in the neighborhood, he expected to have food stolen from him, but it had not yet happened.

My meeting with the pharmacist was a little more fruitful. Someone had stolen a bottle of phosphorus from him, a medicine used to cure memory loss. Who would take the medicine? And why?

I also spoke briefly with a number of other townsfolk: a postman, a peddler, and a goldsmith... As all three spend much time on the roads, I had hoped they might have some information. But no one had seen Selden anywhere.

As for the legend of the Hound of the Baskervilles... I must report that no one wants to talk about it.

They speak only of a huge, monstrous beast with glowing eyes... It spreads such fear across the county that one would struggle to find anyone bold enough to cross the moor at night.

A seamstress, nicknamed "Old Mary" warned me: "Do not step foot there. Danger rises out of the earth itself."

Quaerebatur hos increpabat armorum ma

POST OFFICE

Please Write Distin

From: SHERLOCK HOLMES

DO NOT, UNDER ANY CIRCU
LET SIR HENRY GO TO THE

Jeweler

GRIMPEN, 1888

Chapter V
THE GREAT MOOR OF GRIMPEN

The old woman had piqued Watson's curiosity. So, instead of going back to Baskerville Hall by the road, he decided to cut across the moor. He had been walking for a good half hour when, suddenly, thick fog rose up and hung over the moor like a coat.

The fog was so thick that he could not see, walking only to the sound of the cawing of some invisible crows.

Such a setting did not inspire in him any confidence.

Suddenly he could feel the ground giving way beneath his feet. Quicksand! Watson was completely stuck fast in the ground. The more he fought back, the more his body sank into the slimy mud.

"Stop! Don't struggle!" shouted a man emerging from the mist.

The stranger grabbed a thick branch and reached it over to the poor Watson, who was beginning to suffocate.

"Grab this! Quick!"

With great effort, and in spite of the heavy mud on his clothes, Watson managed to drag himself out of the trap.

"Whomsoever you are, sir, I owe you my life. I thank you with all my heart."

"Stapleton, Jack Stapleton. I live on the Merripit farm, not far from here. You are Dr. Watson, I presume."

"You know me?"

"I am an old friend of Dr. Mortimer. I was at his house when you visited the village, and he pointed you out from his window. When I left him, I saw you walk toward the moor. I know the area quite well, so I thought I could make myself useful. But you are shivering! My house is less than a mile from here. Come, and let's warm you up."

"Gladly. I am very grateful to you."

"Let me introduce to you the great moor of Grimpen. One step in the wrong direction, and you are dead for sure. Even during the dry season, it is dangerous to walk here. Since it rained so heavily over the past weeks, it is even more so. A horrible place, if truth be told."

"But you know how to cross it?"

"Yes. There are some ways that are accessible to an agile man. I have discovered them through the course of patient exploration."

"But why come to such a hostile place?"

"It's a mortal trap for hikers passing through, but a paradise to a naturalist like me. I'll never grow tired of this moor! You have no idea how many treasures it contains. It's so big, so mysterious...

"Did you know, for instance, that our ancestors from the Paleolithic Period also lived in this area?

"And, in the Neolithic Period, humans used this spot for their religious ceremonies. Look at these rocks placed in rows and in circles: druids visited here several times a year, especially for solstices. Some say they used to sacrifice animals. I don't believe it myself. They were much more sophisticated than one might imagine, and it is likely that these stones served another purpose; for instance, tracking the height of the sun and the position of the planets."

Stone-row of Dart

Stone-ro

Jack Stapleton couldn't complete his lesson—an icy wind swept the moor, carrying with it a mysterious moan.

Starting off as a low murmur, it rose and deepened and gained strength, and then it fell again.

Both men stopped as if they had been turned to stone.
"What was that?" exclaimed Dr. Watson, not even attempting to conceal his panic.
Stapleton didn't answer right away. He waited until the sinister call had vanished again in the depths of the earth, where it seemed to have come from.

"But what was that?" Watson insisted.
Stapleton hesitated. He seemed uncomfortable.
"I have heard the noise a number of times before, but never as distinctly as that. People say that it is the Hound of the Baskervilles demanding his prey!"

Dr. Watson looked around the moor, desperately searching for where the ghastly moan could have come.
"You are an educated man, Mr. Stapleton. And, what is more, a naturalist. I take it you don't believe these ghost stories about a hound any more than I do! What do you suggest is making these bizarre sounds?"

"Nature sometimes produces curious noises: the wind between rocks, tree trunks moaning, or whatever else."
"No! You know full well that was the noise of an animal."
"Perhaps, then, it was a wild pony caught in the quicksand."
"Whatever it was, it was the most frightening noise I have ever heard!"
"All in all, this part of the country is rather bizarre and frightening, Dr. Watson.

"But here we are: this is my home."

Stone-row of Dartmoor

Chapter VI
THE STAPLETONS OF MERRIPIT

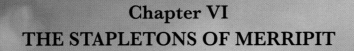

The two men finally arrived at the Merripit farm. The house had always had this name, a relic of its first owner. A small orchard surrounded it, but, like everywhere else on this bleak, wind-battered moor, the trees were sickly and knotted.

"Quickly, do come in, Dr. Watson, and warm up next to the stove. My sister will fix us a nice cup of tea."

Leaning from the window, Stapleton called to his sister in a suddenly commanding and menacing voice.

"Beryl! Beryl! Where has she gone now?"

Then, turning to Dr. Watson:

"Forgive me, I don't know where my sister has gone. She tends to disappear!"

And he left the room still calling the same name:

"Beryl! Beryl!"

Left to his own devices, Watson let his eyes roam around his host's home. It was an odd farm, to say the truth, with its walls and furniture completely covered with items collected from all over the world. He was lost deep in his thoughts when, suddenly, a breathless young woman entered the room.

It was Beryl Stapleton. Without so much as an introduction, she said to him:

"Go away! Go back to London immediately!"

Watson was extremely surprised at these words. After a moment's hesitation, he replied:

"And why exactly should I go back to London immediately?"

"I cannot tell you, but your life is at stake. For the love of god, do as I say! Leave this place! Leave, and never set a foot on the moor again! Don't you know this land is cursed for all those who carry your name?"

Then, upon recognizing the voice of her brother calling:

"Silence! Here comes my brother! Not a word of what I just said!"

Jack Stapleton returned and made no effort to hide his anger.

"Beryl! Where were you? Can't you see that our guest is freezing?"

"I was just offering a cup of tea to Sir Henry..."

"Sir Henry? But whom did you think you were talking to?"

Confused, Beryl Stapleton turned to Dr. Watson:

"Are you not Sir Henry Baskerville?"

"No, miss. I am but his modest friend. Watson, James Watson, at your service, Miss Stapleton."

Watson bowed as politely as he could. Red from embarrassment and unable to say a single word, the young woman left as suddenly as she entered. Jack Stapleton shouted her name twice again, but in vain.

"Please excuse my sister's behavior, doctor. She is used to the company of uncouth men, soldiers, and peasants."

"But, of course. Yourself, Mr. Stapleton, you seem to have traveled a lot."

"Indeed! Our glorious colonial army has allowed me to go on many adventures. I was in Kabul in Afghanistan when we chased Shin Ali away from the throne in favor of Abdul Rahman. Then, the conquest of Egypt, Somalia, and Ethiopia gave me the opportunity to discover Africa. My passion for nature springs from this!"

"So much so that you left the military life?"

"Not completely. At first, I became a naturalist in the Colonial British Office of Khartoum in Sudan. I was in this job for a few years until my parents died, marking the end of my study of African fauna. I then came back to England to take care of my sister."

THE BRITISH COLONIAL

ARMY

"Are you from the region? And if not, why on earth did you choose to settle so close to this desolate moor?"

"The inheritance left to me by my parents was very small. I had to sell their house and settle in Norwich. We led a humble life, Beryl as a maid, me as a gardener. Until fate led me to discover this area, sparsely populated but rich in natural wonders.

"The Merripit farm had been abandoned. We refurbished it, settled down, and became farmers."

"Well, you seem happy enough. But doesn't the isolation affect you?"

"At first it did. But I now have a few acquaintances in the neighborhood. There is Dr. Mortimer, as you already know, and a few other notable people of the area. And I can also flatter myself to say that I won the trust of Sir Charles."

Jack Stapleton paused for a long while, as if honoring the memory of the late Baskerville. Then, pulling himself together:

"On that note, when will we be able to pay our respects to the new Lord of Baskerville?"

"Sir Henry has already told me he wishes to meet his neighbors. The manor is open every evening from 4 o'clock."

"In that case, I think that my sister and I shall pay him a visit tomorrow!"

And a few
days later...

My dear friend on the other side of the Atlantic,

I hope this letter finds you as well as when we last met in New York. I will soon tell you all about my crossing to Europe, and how, through the inheritance I told you about, I find myself caught up in the saga of a dark family curse.

But for now, dear friend, I simply wish to open my heart to you, as I used to do in our youth.

I have recently made the acquaintance of a lovely young woman by the name of Miss Beryl Stapleton. She lives with her brother, Jack Stapleton, and they both came and paid me their respects a few days ago. From the moment I saw her I felt a profound attraction to this young and beautiful woman. And I think I can add that she was as equally taken by me! She is elegant and has an intent stare and soft voice.

Well, is all not well? I am sure you are asking.

Alas, no. I quickly discovered that her brother does not like this mutual attraction, to the point where, almost rudely, he ended the visit and they left in a hurry.

The next day, I invited Miss Stapleton for a cup of tea in the winter garden, without her brother's knowledge. We were pleasantly chatting when he burst into the room. Red with anger, his voice trembling, he grabbed his younger sister and forbade her to return. And away they went, without as much as a good-bye!

I will confess, I do not understand his behavior.

Am I not an excellent marriage prospect for this Stapleton, who lacks both title and money?

Would not a loving and devoted brother be, one day, pleased to call his sister Lady Baskerville?

I am determined to see Miss Beryl again, but we will have to be more careful from now on.

Mr. Jeremy Smith
231 Lafayette Avenue
New York
United States of America

H. Baskerville

Chapter VII
A LIGHT ON THE MOOR

A few days passed without anything troubling the peaceful sleep of all the residents at Baskerville Hall. Until one night, as Dr. Watson was once again struggling to fall asleep, he heard footsteps, light, but very distinct, coming from the house's attic. Who could be walking up there in the dead of night?

Watson quietly made his way to the attic. But as he reached the top of the ladder, there was no one to be seen! Despite this, there were signs that the attic had regular visitors, and had had one recently! The proof? A lamp, still lit, sitting next to the open window! It must have been a signal for someone outside. Perhaps Sir Henry and Miss Stapleton were using this as a means to communicate secretly?

Watson also found a half-open trunk filled with clothes and a stash of food.

Watson was so engrossed in his investigation, a detail startled him: what he thought was a reflection of his own candle in the glass on the right window was, in fact, another light! A light outside, somewhere near the ruins of the old abbey.

There was no mistaking it: someone was sending signals from outside, and someone inside the manor was answering them!

My Lord, thought Watson immediately. Sir Henry must be secretly meeting Miss Stapleton in the ruins of the abbey!

Immediately, Sherlock Holmes's firm instructions came to mind: "Do not, under any circumstance, let Sir Henry go to the moor alone."

*Do not, under any circumstance,
let Sir henry go to the moor alone stop*

Watson quickly went back to his room. A few
moments later he was fully dressed and putting
on his bowler hat. He checked that his colt was
loaded and, in spite of the fog, rushed out on the
moor to look for Sir Henry.

Guided by the light, Watson hurried to the spot where he thought their meeting had been arranged. But it was deserted. There was no one there at all. A deadly silence hung across the moor…

Suddenly, he heard a deep growl that seemed to come from the very depths of the earth.

Watson recognized it at once: it was the same growl he had heard a few days before when he was with Jack Stapleton. The words echoed in his head: "It is the Hound of the Baskervilles demanding his prey…"

The growl then turned into a ferocious roar, the predatory howl of a true beast. At once, Watson spotted a man, visibly panicked, hurtling through the ruins. He recognized Sir Henry by his cape!

"NO! Sir Henry! NOT THAT WAY!" yelled Watson toward the vanishing silhouette.

But his warning was lost in the night. A final roar, a terrified cry, a heavy crash, the gasp of someone in agony… and everything was silent again.

Terrified, Watson barely dared to move when a familiar voice made him start.

"Good evening, Watson! An eventful night, is it not?"

For a few seconds, the doctor was astounded. That cool, incisive, ironic voice…it could belong to one man and one man only! It was Sherlock Holmes, who had popped out like a jack from his box!

Watson set aside the whirling questions his brain demanded answers to, and hurried toward Sherlock Holmes.
"Quick, Holmes! We may still be able to save him!"
But Sherlock held back his loyal friend.

"That would be quite useless. We can no longer be of help to the wretch Selden."

Once again, Watson was unable to conceal his surprise.
"Selden? The escaped convict? Is it not Sir Henry who just lost his life in such tragic circumstances?"
But then, thought Watson, Sir Henry is in great danger, alone in the manor with the Barrymores!
"Good Heavens! The Barrymores!"
Sherlock Holmes cut him off again.
"I assure you, Sir Henry has nothing to fear from the Barrymores. Now, my dear friend, I think I owe you some explanations."

In fact, Holmes had arrived in Devonshire just three days after Watson and Sir Henry! Unknown to everyone, he had hidden away in the ruins so as to keep watch on the moor as discreetly as possible. Only Grimpen's postman knew: he made sure to bring food to Holmes and to hand over the reports Watson was sending to him.

With his usual cunning, it did not take Sherlock Holmes long to establish that another man was hiding out in the ruins: Selden, escaped convict.

Sherlock Holmes also discovered a network of underground tunnels, dating from the time the abbey was built and connecting to several sites in the ruins, including the well.

Upon hearing growls and spotting a dog's collar and some chewed bones, he came to the conclusion that an animal was being hidden somewhere in the tunnel.

More worrisome still: Sir Henry's slipper, the one stolen in London, was found here. The animal must have been trained to recognize Sir Henry's smell!

Another mystery was a model of false teeth, made to resemble the jaws of a huge wild animal…

Chapter VIII
THE BARRYMORES' SECRET

Back at the manor, Sherlock Holmes and Watson found Sir Henry and the Barrymores out of bed and fully dressed. An hour ago, Dr. Watson's hasty departure followed by the howls on the moor had put the manor on high alert. As the agonized noises reached Baskerville Hall, they reminded Sir Henry of the horrible threat still weighing on his shoulders. This explained his look of clear relief when he saw it was Sherlock Holmes entering at the door.

"You, here, Mr. Holmes? I cannot tell you how much your presence is a comfort to us! But tell us, what just happened on the moor? Where were those beastly howls and terrified cries coming from?"

"About the supposed beast, I can tell you not a thing, I am afraid. The night is too dark and we could see nothing."

"But those cries? They came from a human being, I presume?"

"It is true. And the man is dead. It was Selden, the escaped convict."

Holmes's tale was interrupted by a sharp cry, followed by a long moan.

"Oh my god, is it true?"

"Mrs. Barrymore, there is no doubt about the fate of the poor man."

"My brother! My poor brother!"

They all turned to Sir Charles's servant. With eyes full of tears and in great distress, she held tightly to her husband's arm.

"Your brother was…"

"The escaped convict, yes sir. Selden, the criminal everyone was after."

"Mrs. Barrymore, we understand your pain, but you owe us some explanations."

"Yes, sir. My maiden name is Selden, and Robert was my youngest brother. We spoiled him so much when he was a child that he ended up believing that everything was due to him. As a teenager, he got involved with the wrong boys. He broke my mother's heart and dragged our name into the dirt. From crime to crime, he sank further and further, only God's mercy keeping him from severe punishment…"

"But to me, sir, he was still the little boy with curly blond hair that I used to cuddle."

"His presence on the moor was, therefore, due to your connection to Baskerville?"

"Yes, sir. When he escaped, he knew that my husband and I would not refuse him help. He turned up here one night, crazed and famished, the police in hot pursuit. What else were we to do? We welcomed him, fed him, and comforted him. Then you arrived, sir…. Robert left to hide out on the moor and we came up with a way to communicate…"

"Now I understand!" exclaimed Watson. "The light in the attic, the light on the moor in the middle of the night! So, it was you and him?"

"Yes, sir. It was our way of making sure he was there. If he answered our signals, my husband went out to take him water, some meat and bread, and some old clothes that had belonged to Sir Charles. Every day, we hoped he would leave. But now, he's gone for good… This is the whole truth. If anyone is to blame, it isn't my husband, it is solely me."

"Nobody is blaming you for aiding your brother," said Sherlock Holmes. "Though, on reflection, this was a dangerous scheme and one which has ended badly."

"But tell us how this man died. Is there a connection between his death and the dreadful legend we are all so familiar with?"

"An indirect connection, certainly, Sir Henry. There is, indeed, a frightful animal on the moor. It is not a big cat or a monstrous beast, but its presence and its howls were enough to scare Selden to the point where he broke his neck falling down the ruins."

"But what is the animal?"

"For the time being, I'm afraid I cannot say more. It is getting late and we all need rest, gentlemen.

"Moreover, we ought to leave Mrs. Barrymore to her grief. I suggest we retire to our rooms."

And all went to their rooms.

Chapter IX
THE CHURCH OF CROW HILL

Two hours of sleep was enough for Sherlock Holmes to recover his energy, his clarity, and his curiosity! Dawn had just broken when he slipped silently from his room and out of Baskerville Hall. He headed directly to the small church of Crow Hill, surrounded by mist and thrown around by the wind.

It was the parish of Reverend Kircher, a friendly man who cared for the Devonshire archives, dating all the way back to England's invasion by William the Conqueror!

When Sherlock Holmes explained the purpose of his visit and asked to consult the archives of the Baskerville family, the Reverend Kircher reacted most surprisingly:

"I am delighted to make your acquaintance, Mr. Stapleton. The visits of your charming sister are a great pleasure and an honor for me, but I am pleased to at last put a face to the name!"

"I am very sorry to disappoint you, Reverend, but I believe you are mistaken. My name is Holmes, Sherlock Holmes."

"The famous detective? Well, this is odd!"

"It certainly is, but how did you come to confuse me for Jack Stapleton?"

"Until now, it is only Miss Stapleton who has come to consult the archives, on behalf on her brother."

"I see. So, you never met her brother. Well, I too would like to have a look at these documents."

Baskerville family

The collection of records included several volumes of deeds, documents, chronicles, manuscripts, and private letters.

Sherlock Holmes made himself comfortable at a desk and, in the silence of the isolated church, began looking for clues, for the details that might seem insignificant but would, in fact, shed light on this most puzzling of investigations.

Pages went by, one after the other, revealing family secrets and feuds. Five centuries of history, land ownership, forest sales, bravery in the field of war, pettiness, generosity, and jealousies.

After much research, a lead began to appear to the detective, clearer and clearer. And soon, he found the key to the whole riddle, as plain and obvious as the printed words beneath his magnifying glass...

The next few days were perfectly calm in Devonshire. The sky, heavy with mist, let through only a flat, gray light, and evening fell faster every day.

Inside Baskerville Hall, the Barrymores carried out their duties in silence and were gloomier than ever because of their bereavement and difficulties in arranging Robert Selden's funeral.

Dr. Mortimer was scarcely more talkative on the many occasions he visited Sir Henry, whom he examined with great care and toward whom he showed almost motherly attentions.

Sir Henry, on the other hand, seemed in high spirits. He was visited daily by Beryl Stapleton, for whom his passion was obvious. Charming and full of smiles, she had nevertheless to deal with the presence of her brother during her visits to Baskerville. One afternoon, when Sir Henry was disappointed he could not meet her alone, she quickly whispered into his ear: "Let's meet one night on the moor."

As for Sherlock Holmes, he spent most of his days pacing the moor. The detective found that this solitary walk across the desolate landscape greatly aided his concentration and his powers of deduction.

His thoughts revolved around the information he discovered in the archives at Crow Hill. Most especially, one crucial detail had sparked an extraordinary turn in the course of his investigation: an unexpected name had jumped out of the Baskerville family tree.

In a hurry, Watson and Holmes checked that their guns were loaded and rushed on to the moor toward the ruins.

"Quick, Watson! Let's go through the tunnels!"

Chapter X
THE MARK OF THE BASKERVILLES

Holmes sat down with Watson and Mortimer over a cup of tea and some scones to share his discovery.

"Let us be frank. Not one of us can truly believe in the existence of a ghostly hound that haunts the moor and tears apart reckless passersby. The deaths that have taken place are not mere coincidences: the victims are dead because they were presumed to be Baskervilles: rightly, in the case of Sir Charles, but wrongly in the case of the wretch Selden."

"What do you mean? What is the connection between Sir Charles and the convict?"

"There is no connection at all for a human brain, of course. But animal instincts don't work in the same manner. Remember what Barrymore told us: when Selden was still living on the moor, he took him food but also old clothes that once belonged to Sir Charles. These clothes still carried the smell of their late owner: an animal trained to recognize that smell would be unable to check the identity of the person. If it is trained to howl, it howls. If it is trained to attack, it attacks."

"Then, can we say Selden was killed by mistake?"

"Absolutely! He was threatened by an animal trained to attack the Baskervilles, and the Baskervilles alone.

"The question remaining, therefore, is who trained the beast? Who is trying to hurt the Baskervilles?"

"My conviction was slowly built upon the foundations of some indisputable facts:

The person who would want to eliminate successive owners of Baskerville Hall must have their sights on the Baskerville fortune. Yet that person could only make a legal claim to that fortune, an inheritance claim, if you will…"

"But there is no heir after Sir Henry!"

"Yes! There is one, and he is behind the whole affair. It is the man we know by the name of Jack Stapleton."

"The naturalist from the Merripit farm? How on earth?"

Sherlock Holmes then proceeded to explain that he had found the name Stapleton in the Baskerville family tree and that this led him to suspect Jack Stapleton of desiring to claim his right to the inheritance. But how could he prove it?

"Look at these family portraits! All the Baskervilles have a birthmark on various parts of their bodies, and this has been so forever. Dr. Mortimer, did you notice that kind of mark on Sir Charles and Sir Henry?"

"Absolutely! Charles had one on his hand and Sir Henry on his shoulder!"

"My Goodness!" exclaimed Watson, "Stapleton has the same mark! I noticed it when he saved my life in the quicksand."

"But none of this proves that he did anything."

"This is true," replied Holmes. "We are going to set a trap and send Sir Henry into the lion's den. This way, we'll catch Stapleton red-handed, along with his sister who is also in on the plan."

"Let us explain all of this to our friend, and hope that he has enough nerve to participate. Mrs. Barrymore, would you please ask Sir Henry to join us?"

"Sir just went out with Miss Beryl through the small door that leads on to the moor."

"So it is tonight! They plan to kill him!"

"Do you really believe…?"

"Of course! Let's not waste a single second!"

In the midst of the ruins, under the moonlight, Henry Baskerville and Beryl Stapleton looked to be swept up in a moment of great romance. Blinded by his passion, Sir Henry was about to declare his love to the young woman. But to his great surprise, Beryl rejected his advances...

"This is the place I wanted to show you, Sir Henry. And now, I'll show you my secret..."

The young woman was now unrecognizable: where she had once been soft and tender, she was now aggressive and threatening.

"Ah! Ah! Ah! You are caught in the trap, Sir Henry! Just like Sir Charles before you! The old fool also fell for me! And he also came out with me on to the moor in the middle of the night, despite the dire warnings of the legend. Well, just like Sir Charles before you, and just like your ancestor, the evil Hugo, you now must face...

... THE HOUND OF THE BASKERVILLES!"

At these words, a terrifying creature emerged from the depths of the night. It was a hellish beast! Its muscular body was blacker than the blackest night, its paws were enormous...but most terrifying of all was its glowing, red eyes. Worse still, its muzzle was wide open, revealing monstrous fangs.

Scared witless, Sir Henry couldn't move or shout for help. His heart was beating wildly and he was breathing heavily, gasping for air. He was going to faint and collapse, just like Sir Charles before him.

But the beast was not counting on the intervention of Sherlock Holmes and Dr. Watson.

At the end of the confusing tunnels that wound beneath the ruins, they emerged right into the middle of the drama. Pointing their guns at the beast, they fired together.

Shot through the heart, the huge animal collapsed. Seeing that their plan had failed, the Stapletons ran out onto the moor. Sherlock Holmes rushed after them while Watson remained to comfort Sir Henry, who was completely terrified.

The beast lay dead on its flank. Even in the moonlight, it was difficult to identify: Was it a dog? A wolf? A hyena? Perhaps some hybrid beast that Stapleton had brought back from Africa. Watson noted that it had been fitted with fake teeth, fake claws, and that its mouth and eyes had been painted with phosphorus.

This is how Jack Stapleton, the clever naturalist with a heart of stone, had transformed an ordinary creature into a nightmarish devil that seemed to come straight from hell...

The Stapletons knew the moor better than anyone, but the night, the mist, and the fear conspired to confuse them. They tripped and sank in the quicksand. Sherlock Holmes soon arrived on the scene...

But it was too late! He could do nothing to save them.

Chapter XI
EIGHT MONTHS LATER

Several cases, some of them dark and tragic, had all but erased the memories of Baskerville from the busy life of Sherlock Holmes.

One summer evening, he was enjoying a few peaceful moments in his Baker Street office in the company of his loyal friend, Watson, while playing some melodies on his violin.

The Devonshire case came to mind as they sipped the delicious brandy Sir Henry had sent to the detective shortly after the conclusion of the investigation.

"Have you had any news recently?" asked Watson. "All I know is from a few letters I exchanged with my colleague, Mortimer. I know that the Barrymores left Baskerville Hall, as they had planned to do, and opened up a shop not far from Grimpen. The Stapletons' farm is for sale but still hasn't found a buyer. Though that is no mystery."

"For my part," Holmes replied, "I received a letter from Sir Henry informing us of his wedding and honeymoon in France. I believe you know his wife. By now, the happy couple is probably back at the manor, which is under the protection of the hound of the Baskervilles."

"The protection of the hound of the Baskervilles? By God, Holmes, what do you mean?"

"You'll understand my meaning if you read his letter."

Deauville

Grand Hôtel de Normandie

Dear Mr. Holmes,

It is with great pleasure that I write this letter to my benefactor, without whom I would probably no longer be in this world.

Thanks to you, I am alive. And I am happy to let you know that I am now marrying Miss Marguerite Pinson, the young woman I had met aboard the Lily-Jane between Southampton and Portsmouth!

We are currently finishing our honeymoon in her beautiful country, France! I've discovered the thousand marvels of Paris, as well as Normandy and this new trend that is called sea bathing. What a striking contrast to the mist of Devonshire, and yet we are returning in a few weeks!

The prospect of once again seeing Baskerville Hall still caused me panic until not so long ago, as the painful episode we shared persisted in haunting me, even in my dreams. However, I am now at peace, and I am certain that, having expelled our frightful neighbors, it will now be a happy and cheerful place. And I am also counting on our "Hound of the Baskervilles" to protect us!

Do not be alarmed! I merely mean the friendly Dalmatian that my wife and I recently acquired.

Gratefully yours,
Your devoted friend,

H Baskerville

Plage du Grand Hôtel de Normandie - 1889

"Elementary, my dear Watson!"

THE END

Our story has now come to an end! We hope you enjoyed
this Playmobil interpretation of the novel by Sir Arthur
Conan Doyle. Several modifications were made, just as a film
or a play will take some liberties in adapting a novel!

Our warmest thanks go out to Cécile L'Hermite, Stéphane Drilhon,
Isabelle Coletta, Bruno Berard, Murielle Zammit, Norbert Plaine, and
Véronique Meas. Such levels of kindness, help, and support for what is
now more than ten years can only come from dear friends. A loving
thought also goes out to Jean-Louis Michaud-Soret.
Kindest thanks again to Iris Herold and Andrea Schauer for their
many votes of confidence.

Judith
Lili-Jane
Harpo

Many thanks also to the artists who lent their
talents to the creation of some of the settings and
characters: Richard Blim, a.k.a. FanToyRichard,
created the castle, the ruins and the moor.
Michael van Hove, a.k.a. Macgayver, and Lydia
Zunft are behind the reconstruction of Victorian
London and of the steamboat. The policeman
was created by Malone. The open, two-wheeled
carriages, double-decker buses, and coaches were
realized by Emma).

Thanks also to Lazoute for his "Occupations
1900" set and Paulio for his precious castle gate.

Thanks to all! You can find these "friends" and
their Playmobil worlds on Facebook.

A knowing wink to La Muela...

By the same author:

Explore some of the most exciting places around the world in this Playmobil adventure!

Quarto is the authority on a wide range of topics.
Quarto educates, entertains and enriches the lives of our readers—
enthusiasts and lovers of hands-on living.
www.quartoknows.com

© 2015 Quarto Publishing Group USA Inc.
Published by Walter Foster Jr.,
an imprint of Quarto Publishing Group USA Inc.
All rights reserved. Walter Foster Jr. is trademarked.

6 Orchard Road, Suite 100
Lake Forest, CA 92630
quartoknows.com
Visit our blogs @quartoknows.com

Translated by Marion Serre.

© 2013 by geobra Brandstätter GmbH & Ko. KG
® PLAYMOBIL
www.playmobil.com
sous licence de BAVARIA SONOR, Bavariafilmplatz 7 , D-82031 Geiselgasteig.

© Casterman, 2013
www.casterman.com

Casterman Editions
47 Cantersteen, boite 4
1000 Bruxelles

Printed in China
10 9 8 7 6 5 4 3 2
L.10EIFN001870.C002